FINDING
BEAUTY
IN AND OUT

CONFIDENCE - SELF-LOVE - TRUE SELF

Cleanne Lynn Johnson

Copyright

© 2024 by Cleanne Lynn Johnson

ALL RIGHTS RESERVED.

Published in the United States of America.

Name: Cleanne Lynn Johnson, author.

Title: Finding Beauty In And Out

Confidence – Self-love – True Self

Subjects: Self-Help / Self-Esteem / Motivational Self-Help / Personal Transformation / Self-Improvement.

ISBN: 979-8-3507-2779-1 (paperback)

www.cleannejohnson.com

1

Do we possess our true self from birth or gain it through life experiences? Do our parents and peers influence us to validate our true self? When a baby is born up to seven years, they are like sponges, absorbing everything around them and emulating others' actions and words. When young children express themselves, they repeat words until they feel more confident. Are they being their true self? Children shouldn't care about their voice or others' opinions. If it's a bad word, they don't know until someone tells them not to repeat it. Does our true self develop as we grow in our environment, or do we carry our true self from the time we are babies?

I remember a friend's mom telling her how impolite she was as a little girl and now she is an adult and still discourteous. Another one of my friends as a teenager was a quiet introvert, and now she is talkative as an adult. It's astonishing that it's the same person. Can we attribute the first friend's impoliteness to her environment? Did the second friend's environment cause her to shift from being an introvert to an extrovert? Which friend is showing their true self in this situation? I would describe them both as fearless in embracing their true selves.

While the environment plays a significant role in shaping one's true self, it's up to the individual to be authentic. We desire authenticity, but fear judgment when revealing our true selves. We strive to impress others and convince them that our outward behavior and appearance reflect our true self. We display many personalities that perplex both individuals and us—

acting not for the camera, but for life, but if we just act when the camera is around, and feel good about it, when the camera stops rolling, what happens to our true self? How can others perceive our state of being?

When you live as your true self, it is a rewarding experience for both you and others, as it signifies self-approval.

Independence entails not relying on others' opinions and living your life for yourself, not for others. Realizing our true self leads to boldness and courage. Some people express their true selves, while others wait for the opportune moment. When we are young, we speak our minds and are unbothered by others' opinions, but as we age, society influences us to conform to acceptance. True self doesn't seek inclusion in the group. Articulating your real self is hard and demanding in today's society. If you express yourself you're in danger of being canceled. Most individuals are not being true to themselves, instead putting on a facade and saying what others want to hear, even if it causes them suffering. Your true self is expressed through your thoughts and ideas. What's the purpose of wanting to keep that hidden?

Embrace your true self, for there is only one version of you. When you embrace your true self and disregard others' opinions, it unlocks a whole new level of self-belief. The manifestation of your true self lies in self-belief and not seeking validation from others. To truly be yourself, you must first love and accept who you are. Your true self is unattainable. Despite some pretending, your true self is revealed when you reach a point of self-love. It initiates from within oneself.

Children are fearless in expressing their emotions, which is why they are so brave. The moment the child has negativity thrown at them, the true self goes into hiding. The child is reluctant to disclose their feelings because they are ashamed and embarrassed. Our fear of responding arises when someone shares beliefs contrary to our own. We isolate ourselves, refusing to reveal our true selves to others. Your true self is not demonstrated by cursing, disrespecting, or fighting others. Demonstrating authenticity involves sharing your perspective, even if it contradicts someone else's beliefs.

People who don't know your true self may see you as self-centered and arrogant when you embrace your authentic self. It has the capacity to give a false impression.

At what age do we become our authentic selves? Sharing your real identity undermines age limitations. Some people carry their true self from a child until they expire, while others learn the true self along the way. It is crucial to know that being brave and believing in yourself will affect how you present your true self to the world.

QUESTIONS

1. Who I am?

2. How do I activate my true self?

3. Does my true self make me happy?

2

"Getting in touch with your true self

must be your first priority."
Tom Hopkins

How can we establish a connection with our true self? How can we make it our primary focus and fully embrace it? Self-love is the initial stage in understanding your own identity, for without self-love, discovering your true self takes a long time. Our true self is revealed when we are deeply in love with ourselves. The way we carry ourselves is evident in our mannerisms, actions, and speech. The way we walk, our charisma, and how we treat others reflect our true self. When you love yourself, that prevents you from harming others as you recognize your reflection in them. When you love yourself, you remain unaffected by negative comments because you know your true worth.

Understanding your identity and purpose is essential for a long, fulfilling life. Our arrival on this earth is not a coincidence. There's a purpose for all of us. Some individuals die without ever discovering their purpose, while others mistakenly use ineffective methods to search for it.

Other creatures are aware of their purpose. The salmon, when it reaches a certain stage in its young life, moves downstream and interacts with other salmon and fish. When its job is done and it is time for the main purpose of its life, it swims upstream to lay its eggs, then dies. The salmon's ability to know its purpose is a result of the creator's programming data in the salmon's DNA. Are humans inherently programmed to know our purpose on Earth? Is that something placed in your DNA by the creator, or do we struggle to find our purpose, leading to a scattered and unfocused approach?

Parents often determine the purpose of their children from an early childhood. Most children are raised to believe they should be a certain profession based on what their parents desire. The salmon wasn't told to swim downstream and then when it's mature to swim back upstream and lay eggs.

Humans are the only creatures that tell others their fate and their destination—what they should and shouldn't do. A child's life can turn into a living hell if they don't want to pursue the profession chosen by their parents. If the child fails to please the parents, the relationship usually suffers. Some children have learned to please their parents by living their parents' dreams for them rather than connecting with their true self. They are in touch with the parents' true self, not theirs. Some of these adults are troubled and live double lives.

I know a person who was given an ultimatum: become a doctor or pay for their own tuition if it isn't medicine. She chose medicine and now she is the unhappiest physician I have ever seen. The lack of kindness towards the patient, constantly complaining, and showing disinterest in being there. Finally, at the age of forty-five, she immersed herself into her love for singing, forming a band, and launching a YouTube channel, thoroughly enjoying this newfound pursuit. She has discovered her true identity and is loving every moment of it.

True abundance lies in embracing your authentic self. The abundance I'm referring to is not just in physical things, but also internal and external, finding happiness within yourself and embracing your journey. Being true to yourself grants you the chance for your opinions to be heard and accepted without criticism and also gives you the freedom to express your voice without fear of judgment. If we look within ourselves, we have the power to create. Remember, we were created by God. So imagine that God took the time to form us, and if we are created in the image of God, he has given us the seal to create mini versions of his masterpiece.

When I was a child, I was bullied at school because of how I looked and my skin color, which caused me to hide my true self. I didn't want to participate in school activities or show my true self because I felt embarrassed and shy. The only time I revealed my true self was when I spent the summer break with my grandparents in the countryside. We would have talent shows, where I performed songs, share stories, and dance for my family. These were the moments that made my childhood the happiest. It was there that I demonstrated my genuine self. It was as if I had been set free, released from a prison cell only in the summer. I didn't feel judged or criticized.

It felt like I had two personas—my authentic self during the summer and a shy me when school resumed. I concealed it very well over the years. Ashamed of my true self, I kept the secret hidden. It took me many years to realize the need to improve myself and to recognize my value. I understood the importance of self-reflection and self-love as key factors in transforming my life and self-esteem. I refused to let others define my identity any longer. Society's opinion of me and how I should look had a strong influence on my upbringing. It took time, but affirmations helped me cultivate self-love.

One train ride with an isolated incident quickly led to me saying affirmations. You may wonder, how does riding the train relate to self-love? That's where it all started. A woman of another ethnicity on the LRT train in Edmonton, Alberta, stared at me, and I felt uncomfortable as negative thoughts rushed through my head—thoughts of being ugly, too black, and not beautiful. I questioned why she was staring at me and if she was mentally unstable.

She gave me a piercing glare for about five minutes, then her mouth gradually opened. "You are beautiful and gorgeous," she said to me with a smile, leaving me astonished. I had never seen or interacted with this woman before. I thought that was an awkward moment. This incident had me examine myself. I went home and looked deep into the mirror at my skin and face. My skin had lacked the admiration and respect it deserved until that moment. The experience of being told you're too dark causes trauma and instills fear, which led me into doubting my worthiness to embrace my true self. To avoid further name-calling, I retreated into a cocoon, keeping my authentic identity hidden.

My life was forever changed by that day. I made it a routine to look in the mirror every day and say to myself, "I am beautiful and gorgeous." I persistently repeated affirmations, including my love for my skin, until I believed them. It took more than ten years to really show my true skin. I became unapologetic about my dark skin. By saying this affirmation daily and sometimes doubting it, I've developed a strong urge to continue affirming.

Your self-perception is determined by the narrative you create. From that day on, I decided to tell myself positive stories filled with joy, peace, confidence, and courage. Don't allow others' perception to define who you truly are. For only you can determine and manifest your true self. Take a leap of faith and begin your affirmation. It will lead you far. Starting off, you won't believe it, but repeating it more than twice a day will increase your belief. If someone tries to tell your story, shut them down or overpower their negativity with positivity to break the curse they're bringing into your life. Be careful what you say to yourself. Your words have the ability to either help you succeed or hinder you. Start your day and continue throughout with positive words to make your day abundant and impactful on others around you. The advice my grandmother consistently gave was to be mindful of how you make your bed, as it affects your sleep.

QUESTIONS

1. Do you see your reflection in others?

2. What story are you telling yourself?

3

"Confidence is the most beautiful thing you can possess."
Sabrina Carpenter

Confidence forms the essence of one's true self, and when you have an abundance of confidence, you're loaded. You don't need approval from anyone. It's like walking down the street naked, and not knowing because you are covered with confidence. Lack of confidence often leads to unsatisfactory results in any endeavor. Some people take time to build confidence, while others have it fostered from childhood. In my story, I had to develop my self-assurance, and the woman on the train exemplified that growth. Don't depend on others to like or love you. Focus on self-encouragement and self-acceptance. Treat others with respect and dignity, just as you want to be treated. Loving yourself is the key to gaining self-confidence. Genuine love for others relies on self-love.

One of my friends, an extrovert, lacks confidence, and I'm amazed to see someone without confidence interact so friendly with others. When she was young, her dad's verbal abuse led her to believe she wouldn't achieve anything in life. Throughout the years, she made efforts to assimilate by adopting a talkative persona and feigning self-assurance.

She came to me one day, sobbing, desperate to learn the secrets of building real confidence. She grew weary of pretending, and it became noticeable. Our initial step was to affirm and learn about her identity.

She hadn't forgiven her dad for the verbal abuse and therefore that was hindering her progress. It was necessary for her to confront him, express her emotions, and forgive him. They met up and had a discussion about it. Her dad revealed that he too experienced verbal abuse from his own father, which he believed was normal fatherly behavior, and passed it on to her. He offered an apology to her and demanded that this evil cycle be broken in her generation. Although she had already forgiven him, she still desired to make the change. She loved herself through the stories she told herself—stories of hope, faith, and encouragement. Her outgoing personality took a different approach, not just engaging in idle chit-chat, but before speaking, she thought of her word choices to express her self-certainty. Life was not the same for her. She found purpose and reward not for others but for herself, embracing herself with love and forgiving her father with no reservations. Granting her father forgiveness enabled her to gain confidence and progress towards self-actualization, choosing not to conform.

How would you respond, if you were in my friend's situation? Would you have the confidence to express yourself so affirmatively? It's paradoxical for a life coach to counsel others while their own life is in disarray. One must engage effectively in life-changing endeavors to make confidence crucial. Confidence acts as a driving force, pushing people to achieve the unimaginable. It's the small voice that reassures you, telling you that you can do it.

How often do we hear that small voice inside? Confidence is a constant companion to the voice.

Confidence is not doubting, and it has no fear. Either you have it, or you don't. It's not possible for something to vanish after you've had it. Experiencing tough days doesn't imply losing your confidence. Confidence persists even on bad days. As I previously stated, it never disappears. Negative comments and hurtful behavior from others can aim to weaken your confidence, causing a minor effect. Confidence has the power to overcome human emotions if you allow it.

Let your confidence rid you of negativity. People will always gossip. It's all about how you react. That's when confidence comes in. Your confidence should not depend on how others perceive you.

Is confidence something you search for? Are you born with it in your DNA, or is it a skill you develop over the years? How do we get confidence? Is it a pursuit or an inherent aspect of our DNA or a product of life's circumstances? No matter how you gained your confidence, it's clear in our daily tasks. A life without confidence is comparable to eating flavorless foods. Confidence is the spice that enriches life.

Do we search on Google for confidence or is it the act of doing? Saying you have confidence is easy, but true confidence lies in executing the task. Anyone can say they can do a task, but are they willing to be uncomfortable to deliver the task? Hearing motivational speakers and accomplished leaders can inspire you to pursue your goals and find people in your circle that can help guide you, pushing yourself to do things that defy your expectations.

Circumstances played a role in the development of my confidence. The woman on the LRT train in Edmonton, Alberta, started my journey toward confidence. Before, I had zero confidence. Being raised in the Caribbean by a single parent who worked tirelessly to meet our basic needs with financial constraints, she couldn't buy top-quality school bags and shoes, so I had to settle for what I got. The bullying I experienced at school, based on my appearance and skin color, shattered my confidence. Despite my low self-esteem crying out for help, I kept a brave face on the outside. During my teenage years, I made the move to Edmonton, Alberta, to live with my dad and his family. It didn't improve my confidence; it made it worse. The environment was different. People didn't look like me and I was afraid of being singled out with name calling. While on the train, a woman of another ethnicity stared at me and said, "You are beautiful and gorgeous." I assumed this was a prank. She looked at me once more and said the same words, "You are beautiful and gorgeous."

I never realized my beauty until a woman of a different ethnicity told me I was beautiful and gorgeous. She smiled at me and got off at the next train stop. I went home and looked in the mirror to see what she saw. I started practicing affirmations and believed it had the power to boost my confidence. The story you tell yourself is what matters, not how others perceive you. My confidence grew through the challenges of hardship, struggles, bullying, and staying committed to my narrative.

Some believe that certain children are naturally confident, while others argue parents can instill confidence in them when negativity arises. When your children do good things, give them praise and rewards, which helps to boost their confidence as they grow, and also encourages them to explore new things. Sprinkle your life with authentic confidence and you will receive the benefits.

QUESTIONS

1. How did you get your confidence?

2. How did that benefit you and others?

4

"A man cannot be comfortable without his own

approval."

Mark Twain

The LRT woman started my confidence because her words compelled me to examine myself and solidify it with affirmation. I had to validate her claims because that wasn't normal for me. Her skin color differed from mine, but she saw beauty in me. She didn't make me feel inferior. However, I couldn't perceive what she perceived. Society had consistently positioned me beneath others for a significant period of my life. The truth becomes challenging to believe when you've been fed lies your whole life. How can one erase and replace the subconscious mind with the right information? In the Caribbean, most individuals are descendants from Africa. When someone of your same complexion, but lighter, insults your darkness, the last thing you expect is for someone with a completely different ethnicity to see beauty in you.

Colorism has left its mark on the world, stemming from slavery. Although it is fading, its remnants still affect the lives of people. As Mark Twain said, you need to approve of yourself. No one else can. Although others can affirm your confidence, you must affirm it to yourself. Telling ourselves the right story can bring tremendous change in our life and the lives of others. The subconscious mind seeks to preserve favorable things to promote physical well-being. Throughout my childhood, I internalized the narratives I heard, convincing myself that I was too dark, ugly, and not tall enough. I'd been telling myself these stories, not realizing they weren't mine but rather other people's opinions of me. I made their opinion my reality and, over time, I created the pain of rejection. This pain was created by me taking these stories and making them a part of me. I was unaware of the importance of self-love. Receiving genuine praise was uncommon for a young girl who looked like me.

I was seven or eight years old, playing with my cousin in the yard, when this woman approached us. My cousin, a year older than me, was light-skinned. The woman told her she was stunningly beautiful right in my presence, and the woman then turned to me and gave me a disgusted look saying to my cousin, "You have beautiful light skin." I was waiting for her to compliment me on my beauty, but it never happened. I was filled with shame. My cousin felt sorry for me, as she could detect the sadness on my face.

I longed to hear that I too was beautiful alongside my cousin, but it didn't unfold. It was strange because the lady who said that was as dark-skinned as me. Reflecting on this incident as an adult, I realized this lady was also criticized for being too dark and, like me, she didn't embrace her beauty. She saw me, and saw herself, and that gave her an unpleasant taste, so in order to validate herself, she had to tell me the same negativity said to her—that she wasn't beautiful and was too dark.

Television rarely featured individuals with dark skin when I was growing up. The ones that were light were always the chosen ones. I recall when the queen visited the island. My class was selected to be in the front to wave to the Queen of England, the head of the commonwealth nations. I was told to stay in the back and rearrange the seating so that the light-skinned children were in the front. Colorism denied me the opportunity to see the queen up close, dehumanizing my soul. That was the norm growing up on the island, in the subconscious, and has been passed down from generation to generation.

It does not foster confidence in children with dark skin because positivity is directed towards light-skinned children. Confidence was something that the dark-skinned individuals had to find. I discovered my confidence when I moved to Canada.

God sometimes relocates you to inspire personal growth and connect you with the right people, like the lady on the train. In my youth, the obstacles and difficulties pushed me towards self-assurance and the quest for meaning in life. I established my approval on a solid foundation. Erasing the junk in the subconscious mind and replacing it with healthy ideas is challenging. It took years of affirmation and positivity for me to reach the level of confidence I have now.

To all the haters out there, if you can't say anything positive, please keep silent to avoid harming others. The lady who told my cousin she was beautiful and didn't acknowledge me, was only acting on what she believed to be true. That's what she had been taught. Children, especially, absorb everything and seek approval from others. So, parents praise your children, tell them positive things to boost their confidence, and don't wait for someone else to plant negativity. Children are always looking for approval and love to keep them motivated. Before you speak, reflect on your words to guide others by instilling self-confidence. Start your children on affirmations. It's a great way to help them feel more confident.

QUESTIONS

1. Have you approved your confidence?

2. Do you believe you can change someone's life with a single impactful sentence?

5

Is your love for yourself inclusive of your mind and spirit, not just your outer appearance? Are you in love with what you see, hear, and touch? Do you enjoy the sound of your own voice? What does it require to be fully content with oneself? It can take years of hard work for some people to learn to love themselves.

As we grow, we develop love for others and what television portrays as beautiful. We are influenced by the media, without realizing it, and can cause harm to ourselves by becoming attached. We imitate others, thinking that will bring us happiness.

In relationships, we are constantly searching for love. A friend of mine was involved in a toxic relationship. Despite her partner's verbal abuse and mistreatment, she claimed he loved her. She was raised in a loving family, enveloped in love. Her dad never subjected her mom or their family to physical or verbal abuse. I was surprised that she was in a relationship with that loser. She refused to leave, constantly making excuses for her boyfriend. A flyer was given to her to attend a session on self-love, and she accepted.

During the meeting, she received instructions to gaze into a mirror and have a conversation with herself, expressing self-love. She considered it stupid. Why did she need to tell herself that? Other people are there to express their love for others, right? It all started as a playful endeavor for her, and in just two months, she noticed a difference. She now has a purpose. She is head over heels in love with herself. Right now, she is traveling the world, making TikTok videos, and embracing her journey of self-love. At the time of our last conversation, she was not dating anyone. First, she had to love herself unconditionally. She was out there, living a life of abundance.

Falling in love with self should be the first secret to anyone's happiness, but it is actually the last. We are kept in the dark about the power of self-love. As a child, I felt insecure about my dark skin and not being pretty enough because of lies and negativity and thinking if I was just a little lighter, I would have passed the beauty standard test. The secret of happiness is something most people must discover by themselves. Putting everyone else first while working, going to school, and taking care of children conceals the secret. I'm not suggesting that you neglect your work, school, or family responsibilities. We prioritize these good things and pay less attention to ourselves. Let's not forget about our well-being and investing in self-care. Without spending time with ourselves, how can we expect to love ourselves? Discover your identity before others define it for you.

I wasn't raised in an environment that admired dark skin. I never received compliments on my beauty or worth. My dark skin made other people nauseous to look at me. Growing up, the culture believed light skin was superior to dark skin, regardless of facial appearance. While colorism was a significant concern, it didn't affect everyone. Individuals with light skin were treated preferentially. It was uncommon to find a teller with dark skin back when I was a child. Now there is a plethora of dark-skinned bank tellers in all the different banks, and it is interesting to observe the change in behaviors and mindsets. People are increasingly aware of their true selves, breaking free from the grips of colorism that plagued their ancestors. This disease of colorism affects the mental, physical, and psychological aspects of individuals and can be passed down to future generations getting embedded in culture.

A friend told me a story about a young woman who was pregnant. Despite her light skin, the father of her child had a dark complexion. The baby inherited the dark skin of her father, and the mother didn't like the fact the baby came out dark skinned. The mother questioned why the child had dark skin. That's deep, my friend. I'm wondering if this mother ever loved her child. She grew up not liking the color of her skin and went on to marry a European. Self-hate can only be reversed by oneself; no one else can do it for you. It's important to have unconditional love for yourself. The hate syndrome given upon her by her mother afflicted this young lady. It would have been better if she had worked on self-love before marrying the European. She was unaware of the secret to true happiness. How do we develop a deep love for ourselves and shield our inner peace from external judgments? Understand who you are, why you exist, and what drives you.

By "who you are," I'm not referring to your professional identity or job role. I'm talking about your character, attitude, perception, discipline, charisma, faith, hope, joy, and true self. That's what makes you fall in love with yourself. That's the key to being happy. When your identity is solely your career, it becomes a disaster; who are you once you retire? When we label ourselves with things that don't endure, we become depressed and uncomfortable. We become enraged with the world because of the detrimental effects of retirement. Most of us feel regret about our past lives. We haven't allowed ourselves to love ourselves. This is the first secret to happiness, both when we're young and as we grow older. Loving yourself is possible at any stage, but it takes time. It takes time for two people who are dating to develop feelings of love. Loving ourselves can take years, especially if we didn't start loving ourselves at a young age, as in my case. Allow yourself to improve and become the best version of you. Don't misunderstand me, I'm not saying you shouldn't have a career. Our dedication to our careers can sometimes surpass our self-care, leading us to work ourselves to the point of burnout. We strive to be the best, but what are you willing to sacrifice for that? Your career will thrive when you prioritize self-love. It's heartbreaking for me, as a dietitian in a nursing home, to witness older adults and hear their stories of regret. If given a second chance, they would want to relive their lives. The bitterness of some older adults is understandable, given their lack of love or knowledge of love. Some prioritize the love they have for their children over themselves. They are now lonely, missing the love they once gave.

According to statistics, older adults have the highest suicide rate. These numbers took me by surprise. The knowledge we gain from society and culture shapes how we perceive things. My grandmother seemed happy to me when I was young. She was always laughing and drinking coffee all day, but as I grew older, I realized she wasn't truly happy. I'm uncertain if she had self-love. I loved her, even though I never asked.

Steps towards self-love:

1. Start affirmations.

2. Do the things you want to do.

3. Don't let others define you.

4. Show up unapologetically.

5. Don't let others' perception of you become your reality.

6. Spend time alone with yourself.

7. Read inspirational and motivational books.

8. Listen to inspirational speakers.

9. Helping others and not expecting anything in return.

10. And most of all, loving God.

These will make you fall in love with yourself, so give them a shot. These are the steps I've followed in my journey of loving myself. Loving yourself is a challenge that requires energy, effort, time, and dedication. Saying, "I love myself," isn't something that happens just once. When you have self-love, your actions should reflect it, such as making time for yourself by saying no to others and yes to yourself.

We find it difficult to prioritize ourselves because we haven't received any guidance on how to do so. It's important to help others, but don't prioritize them over yourself. The key to loving others is loving yourself first. By saying yes to yourself multiple times, you create room to say yes to others. In the process of helping others, it's important for you to prioritize self-care and personal growth.

I have learned to love myself abundantly, disregarding the opinions of haters, as it is none of my concern. Whether you're doing good or bad, people will talk about you. They will find something to say regarding you. You have no control over that. While you can choose to read comments on social media, responding is not obligatory, especially if they're negative. Negative comments can help you grow and prove others wrong, but that's not the aim. Explore the journey of self-love, ignore outside judgments, and embrace your authentic self.

I carried the words of the bullied in my subconscious for years, making them a permanent part of me. I had to erase it, and it was the woman on the train who played the role of my eraser. She was an angel dispatched by God. He understood my perception of myself needed to change because He created me in His image. He wants to prevent His creations from feeling worthless and hating themselves. Imagine an artist who paints to express themselves, only for a critic to come and suddenly dislike it. God affirmed we are fearfully and wonderfully made, but the enemy seeks to undermine our confidence in who we are and what we were.

As a child, I was told that Jesus loves me. The Bible says one thing, but the environment says another. It was difficult to learn to love myself in a new environment where people didn't resemble me. Over the years, Europeans were the symbol of beauty on television, and the majority of Canadians are of European descendent. The woman on the train distorted my belief system, when she said, I was beautiful and gorgeous. The transformation didn't happen overnight when she told me that. Now I am in my forties, and I still tell myself that I am beautiful and gorgeous. To help others with self-confidence, I released my first single titled "I am beautiful and gorgeous every day."

Your reality is shaped by the story you tell yourself. If you haven't been telling yourself the correct narrative, begin now. It's never too late to share the right stories.

Your story in the future can be whatever you want, as long as it enriches your life and helps others. Loving ourselves leads to personal growth and recognizing ourselves in others. It fosters love and a desire for the best in others.

There is a verse in the Bible encouraging people to love their neighbors as they love themselves. The Bible states that if you love yourself, you will love your neighbor just as much. Without self-love, it's impossible to love another. Faking love for someone is merely a reflection of faking self-love. If you love yourself, you can't help but love your neighbor.

Self-love is the starting point of love. When you criticize your neighbor, you're probably criticizing yourself too. Your neighbor is someone other than yourself. People who talk negatively about friends behind their back also do the same to themselves in private. We frequently use phrases like "Silly me" or "I am so stupid" when talking to ourselves, which we intend as jokes, but our minds perceive these phrases as reality. Your self-talk has the power to shape where you end up, so be cautious. Practice self-affirmation in both solitude and social settings. When the mind understands positive conversations, it stores them, preventing negative self-talk. Commence today by expressing one positive self-talk, and progressively introduce additional ones as the days and months go by. As you become more confident, your vibrance will elevate and you'll be in tune with your true self.

There are some positive thoughts you can say to yourself:

- I am powerful.

- I am filled with confidence.

- I am courageous.

- I am beautiful and gorgeous.

- I am loved.

- I am blessed and highly favored.

Repeat these three to four times a day, and in six months, you'll truly believe what you're saying. Your thoughts, whether spoken in solitude or amongst others, have the power to become reality. When you begin to elevate yourself, you will elevate others, too. Happiness lies in loving yourself and others just as much. Love is a gift we all need in our lives, and we all can access it. Make self-love a priority and don't procrastinate. Although it may seem tough initially, perseverance and repeating the process can help you learn to love yourself. Nobody will tell you this secret:

love yourself first, then you can love God and your neighbor. When you love yourself whom you have seen, then you can truly love God whom you have not seen.

When you love yourself and embody self-care, attitude, charisma, hope, faith, and caring for others, people will notice your secret to happiness. Don't be scared to show love to yourself. You have a unique identity. Embracing your individuality makes self-love even more effortless.

6

---

*"He who is not courageous enough to take
risks will accomplish nothing in life."*
Muhammad Ali

I took a leap of faith because of the advice from the lady on the train, choosing to take a risk to improve my life and nurture self-love. The pain I had carried for years was silently begging for assistance, and this woman noticed. She noticed I had the courage to become everything I was meant to be. She recognized there was something remarkable about me. She couldn't resist expressing that I was beautiful and stunning, and that bold action she took ended up altering the course of my life. It's surprising to move to a unique part of the world, only to have a random person who doesn't look like me make a bold statement about my beauty. Throughout the years, this one positive aspect has surpassed all the negativity I encountered as a child.

One of my friends had a fear of public speaking but was fearless in one-on-one conversations. However, anxiety would strike when speaking in front of a crowd. Faced with difficulties, she was unsure of how to overcome it. She bravely signed up for private speech coaching. She got promoted to a management position at her job and got a salary boost. Being a single mom with two kids, she needed the extra money. She had to transform her fears into courage. With the right mindset, she took a risk by engaging in public speaking. She prepared for three months before giving her first public speech. Despite her nerves, she was ready and aced it. Occasionally, we rely on others to guide us on our life's journey. The woman on the train caught my attention, whereas the speech coach influenced my friend. Your support system could be your family or someone who sees your true capabilities. The path of bravery is a thrilling adventure. The journey is full of unknowns and surprises. Having the belief in something through self-repetition is an act of bravery. Keep telling yourself positive stories, even if you can't see the positivity now.

Your subconscious mind will believe whatever you feed it. The remote control is in your hands. It is possible to mold and reposition your mind to be in your favor. Picture a potter using a wheel to create a mug. The potter's wheel represents the stories you tell yourself, while the clay symbolizes your mind. By consistently telling yourself the right stories, you can mold that lump of clay into a usable mug. The clay may never form into a mug if you constantly tell yourself negative stories. The starting point might deviate from its intended purpose as a mug.

Taking risks is a constant part of our lives. Every morning, leaving home involves a certain level of danger. It's unclear if you'll come back, be it by train or strolling down the street. We take risks without even realizing it. When we encounter something unfamiliar, we perceive it as a threat. Taking a tremendous risk is like stepping out of your home in the morning—it can have positive or negative outcomes. Opening a business after leaving your nine to five job takes courage, even though the outcome is unknown. To me, having courage means being willing to take risks. Bravery in life lies in taking risks, whether familiar or unfamiliar. The false narratives we have ingrained in ourselves cloud our perception of courage. If someone tries to share a story to uplift us, we quickly shut them down to maintain our ignorance. We're so comfortable in our own vomit that we don't want anyone to tell us otherwise.

The negative narratives I experienced as a child have stayed with me, shaping my life and hindering my self-love. Although the woman praised my appearance on the train, I couldn't accept it because the bullies' perception of me had already affected my subconscious. It took me a long time to shape the mug with my pottery wheel. On certain days, I struggled to believe in my beauty and charm, but I persevered in telling myself a particular narrative. The process of creating the mug to my liking was anything but simple, even though it took me a long time.

During childhood, the brain acts as a sponge, absorbing everything. My subconscious mind had absorbed the bullies' negative words, and it was difficult to flush them out. It appeared I was living the life that the bullies wanted for me. What they said had a major impact on me. Believing their hurtful words about my appearance, I yearned for lighter skin. There were nights when I dreamt of my skin changing and becoming lighter upon waking up. Every time I come across something black, it serves as a reminder of my deep dislike for my dark skin. I don't like things that are black.

Society praised individuals with light skin for their beauty, while disregarding those with dark skin. There was an accident at the grocery store, and a customer, a big dark-skinned woman, asked the sale assistant for help. The sales assistant turned to her colleague just before the woman slowly walked away, and said, "That black thing should know what she wants in the store." Her tone of voice was derogatory when she said it.

Upon hearing, the woman turned as her colleague laughed. It's disheartening that someone would belittle another person in that way. The girl who said "that black thing" had a lighter complexion. The woman reported her to the supervisor, but the colleague claimed she never said that. She got off the hook, scot-free. All the colleagues had a dark skin tone. It's strange how they didn't stand up for the woman.

Colorism is deeply ingrained in our culture. Certain individuals cling to it for comfort, as it has propelled them in society, whereas others strive to dismantle it and create equal opportunities for everyone.

I can relate to the woman's pain because I also have experienced the name calling. I sensed this wasn't the first time the woman had encountered prejudice because of her dark skin. Her skin color is all people focused on.

The young lady who referred to the woman as a black thing, was enduring a disease society had attributed to her. Society ingrained the belief that having light skin was more important, regardless of anything else. Her upbringing led her to believe she could insult anyone, thanks to the authority society had given her.

Upon relocating to Canada, most Canadians had lighter complexions. The thought of being labeled the "black thing" petrifies me, but when the woman on the train called me beautiful and gorgeous, my life changed. Programming my subconscious mind took years, but being in a supportive environment that didn't see my race helped to shape who I am today. It was on that LRT train in Edmonton, Alberta that my courage developed. I allowed the world to define and dehumanize me for many years, stripping me of my dignity and power. The LRT woman affirmation sparked my courage to take risks and pursue my dreams, disregarding others' opinions and creating my brand.

QUESTION

1. What's the biggest risk you have taken?

7

"Believe you can and you're halfway there."
Theodore Roosevelt

The key to achieving your goals, whether physically, mentally, or spiritually, requires belief and faith. No one else can experience the joy of a solo game on your behalf. The responsibility of initiating the belief system falls on you. It doesn't begin operating by itself initially. Belief is essential, but action is equally important to manifest that belief. Despite my initial disbelief, the words spoken to me on the train were proven true through years of personal growth and dedication. It was challenging to begin affirming something to myself that I didn't initially believe. I continued to say it, even when progress was not visible. Molding my mind proved to be a struggle, given the negative comments I received as a child. Each time I uttered a positive affirmation, a negative one would materialize in my mind. It took me years to remove negativity from my subconscious mind and replace it with positive affirmations.

Belief is an important factor in reaching our goals, but without effort and hard work, it remains incomplete. You can convince yourself that you are wealthy by affirming it daily, saying, "I am a millionaire; I am a millionaire," and sit on the sofa all day watching TV. Your belief is pointless, then. To become a millionaire, it's important to set goals for yourself daily, weekly, monthly, and yearly unless you receive an inheritance.

The woman on the LRT train helped me discover my voice to sing my special song. Her support gave me the strength to believe in myself, even when I thought it was impossible. She started me singing my song, not the song of others. I needed to write lyrics that reflected my worth, allowing me to sing a melody with confidence and pride. This song has been on repeat in my head.

The great teacher and Lord, said to the father of the child, "If you can believe, all things *are* possible to him who believe."

He responded, "Lord I believe. Help my unbelief." He asked for help with his doubtfulness, that he couldn't do it alone. The task was so difficult that he had to seek divine help, but he still had faith in his daughter's healing. The power lies within our beliefs. Despite not being able to envision how his daughter would be helped, the master assured him. He found the strength to act on that belief, even when he wasn't completely convinced. When forming beliefs, focus on the positive rather than allowing space for negative beliefs, as they can have an equal effect. For years, he watched his daughter suffer from illness, feeling helpless and in need of encouragement. Jesus came through for him. His words inspired hope in him, compelling him to act. The man only halfway believed, so he pleaded for help in overcoming his disbelief.

The woman on the train instilled belief in me by describing me as beautiful and gorgeous. Recognizing my low self-esteem and lack of shame, she felt compelled to deliver a message to help me unlock my full potential and overcome my past. The journey of rediscovering my childhood and becoming the person I am today began with a stranger's words spoken on a train. I had to fix my mistakes and focus on self-improvement, learning to love myself. The task was far from simple. I had to eliminate the useless thoughts and make room for important ones. It's comparable to switching to a more nutritious diet. The urge to return to the familiar you is hard to resist. I've been carrying the weight of negativity for so long that it has become a part of me, unwilling to let go. I had to shift my mindset and embrace a healthy diet in order to grant myself permission to move on.

Leaving behind toxic chemicals, my mind is focused on the organic. Sometimes I doubt myself, questioning the statement, "I am beautiful and gorgeous," as my mind battles with opposing views. I chanted it, day after day, without sharing it with others, to avoid negativity. Through the years, I've discovered that the longer you're around someone, whether they're honest, it starts to manifest in your behavior and attitude. When you believe someone to be true, they will become that in your eyes. It will become your undeniable fact. Breaking the liar and confronting the truth demands commitment and perseverance. It's as if you must relearn how to walk from scratch, one step at a time. I had to ingest words that felt untrue, learning to digest these words, to change my state of mind.

A freed mind comes with responsibilities that sometimes we are unwilling to take, and when we do take on these responsibilities, our role in the story will definitely change, which is onerous. Sometimes we need to put on a new character to make these changes.

I reluctantly started adopting positive affirmations, not because of personal desire, but because the woman reassured me of their authenticity. In order to prioritize mental health, success, and self-love, we need to eliminate harmful traditional culture that unknowingly negatively affects our minds. I believe that shifting perspective can positively impact self-esteem and increase our capacity to love. A simple word or gesture has the potential to greatly enhance someone's life and bring them true satisfaction. It's up to you to begin the belief. Have faith in your abilities and you can achieve anything you focus on. Belief is something no one else can do for you. Your life can be transformed by simply believing in yourself and staying determined.

8

"Happiness is not by chance but by choice."
Jim Rohn

Making yourself happy is your own priority. No one can do it for you. Happiness lies in embracing your authentic self, showing love to yourself, and engaging in activities that bring you joy. Make the choice to be happy. Repeating positive affirmations has boosted my happiness. I am sharing my narrative, not the narrative others create about me. As a child, I projected happiness outwardly, but internally, I was not content. My subconscious mind held onto negative words and insults that belittled my beauty and criticized my dark skin tone. I counted on words to bring me joy, but when the wrong words were said, it stole away the little happiness I possessed.

Growing up on the island, I believed having light skin was the key to happiness. Television failed to depict people with my skin color as beautiful. When I watched American TV, I realized that African Americans were often given roles of janitors, maids, or thieves in movies. I felt discouraged and less happy when I realized that people with my skin color were only represented in that particular role. Societal standards influenced me to only identify with light-skinned actors, as they were considered more valuable.

In my elementary school, there was an incident where two dark-skinned boys fought because one didn't want to be identified as African after the other mentioned their African origins. Students, even those with dark skin like me, were inventing their own ancestry DNA by falsely claiming European grandparents. It was the norm; some of the students were unwilling to acknowledge that they were of African descent in the Caribbean. Classes didn't cover black history. The extent of my knowledge about black history is the transportation of African slaves to the Caribbean and Christopher Columbus's discovery of the Caribbean. Prior to Columbus' arrival, the land was already inhabited by indigenous peoples.

There were few questions asked by the students, but one boy, whose family followed Rastafarianism, enlightened the class by stating that they were all Africans. Nobody spoke to him afterwards, as you can imagine. They teased him about African people living with animals. The media showed Africa in a negative light, describing it as a place with primitive living conditions, huts, homelessness, and widespread child starvation. On the island, I learned that Africa was the poorest continent, with a history of African slavery. To find happiness, one must embrace the truth, irrespective of others' opinions; it's about considering facts over anything else.

As an adult, I'm realizing that many of the stories I heard about Africa and the world were lies. Reversing all these lies into truth is challenging, causing people to prefer living in falsehoods. My perception of myself would have been altered if I had learned about the amazing aspects of Africa while growing up on the island. I would have self-love, and maybe the name calling would not have happened. Finding out about your background and aspirations brings happiness. The family history was erased because of the negative connotations and evil associations with being black. So my family knows nothing much about African and their culture.

Through an African ancestry DNA test, I discovered that my maternal family hails from the Mandinka tribe in Senegal. The result made me extremely happy. Knowing my place of origin brought me happiness and joy. Many Europeans residing in the Americas take pride in their family's European origins. I have a friend who is third-generation American, but she is so passionate about her Italian ancestry that you would think she recently immigrated to America. I didn't receive that feeling of pride being of African ancestry when I was a child. I had to discover it myself. My friend possesses self-love because she is aware of her identity and background. Understanding where you come from shapes your self-perception.

The availability of social media is enabling more people to find out who they truly are as time progresses. Despite the lingering stigma of light skin, significant progress has been made on the islands. Dark skin is finally receiving the praise it deserves. If you let someone know they are from Africa, they might feel a sense of pride now, compared to when I was a child. People want to be identified with Africa now, as opposed to when I was growing up. Certain individuals are uncovering the truth and attaining the happiness they desire, while others are content with the familiar.

To change a belief, one needs energy and effort, but many people avoid the work and instead choose to remain ignorant and pass it on to their children. Many YouTube content creators from Africa are showcasing the richness and beauty of this abundant continent. It's surprising how the wealthiest continent, in terms of minerals and resources, was depicted as the poorest. I recall the television showing children in mud huts, with massive bellies and flies all over them, without access to water or food. I assumed all of Africa was like that. As an adult, I was in shock when I saw what was on YouTube. Some places were more developed than certain areas in the USA with skyscrapers, gigantic buildings, and modern infrastructure. I couldn't believe this was Africa.

Despite being exposed to countless YouTube videos about Africa, certain individuals remain steadfast in their original mindset. I had the option to find out the truth about my origin and fully embrace it, leading to happiness. Our happiness is our own responsibility; others can't create it for us. Seeking happiness from others often leads to misery when it doesn't pan out, transitioning from one relationship to another in search of happiness, only to realize that it doesn't reside in someone else, but within ourselves.

9

"Be yourself, everyone else is already taken."
Oscar Wilde

We often desire to be celebrities like Beyonce, Jennifer Lopez, and others, oblivious to the fact that they are already taken. Every person has their own unique qualities. There can't be two of Beyonce or of Jennifer Lopez, just like there can't be two of you. There's no greater gift than embracing your true self, not pretending to be someone else just to be liked. Loving yourself means embracing your true, unbreakable, and unstoppable self. Don't allow the opinions of others to hinder pursuit of your dreams. Find joy in your work without comparing it to others. Be fearless and confident, clasping the strength of life, unleashing your genius, and following your instincts.

I was afraid to be myself, because of bullying, because I was unaware of my worth, the bullies claiming I had no value, and my skin color was insignificant. I lacked the knowledge of how to accept my authentic self. Saying my affirmations kick-started my journey to being myself, all because of the lady on the train who ignited that spark in me. During my childhood, I constantly wished to be someone else, idolizing celebrities on television and yearning for a lighter skin tone, aspiring to be a singer and appearing on TV. The singer I loved the most was Tina Turner. "Private Dancer" was my favorite song. I had the desire to become the best version of myself, unapologetically and without hesitation. Being told I needed to be lighter in order to be attractive didn't inspire me as a child. These negative thoughts choked my already fragile self-assurance.

During my infancy, my mom would take me to the health clinic by bus. There on the bus a woman mockingly commented on my appearance, asking my mom how she could have produced such an unattractive baby.

The woman received no response from my mom, who felt embarrassed. Amidst various happenings, another woman on the bus advised the lady to be mindful of the child she was making fun of, as she would one day witness her true beauty. When I was a baby, I had patches of hair on my head, so my mom would put a crocheted hat on my head to avoid people laughing. As a baby, I would remove the hat, which would embarrass her as people laughed. When people are trying to belittle you, it takes resilience, bravery, and a higher power to rescue you from that toxic environment. When I was two, I had so much hair that the lady who used to laugh couldn't help but stop laughing when she saw me. She was astonished and speechless.

In my childhood, I aspired to be like others because I was taught to prioritize physical attractiveness. The mantra stayed with me throughout my teenage years and into adulthood. I had never been complimented on my beauty and attractiveness by someone of a different ethnicity before. That caught me off guard. I think this compliment prompted me to search within myself and work towards personal growth.

By accepting positive thoughts and nurturing the uncontainable you bring about weeds of abundance. Hold on to the positive influences in your life tightly. They will lead you to freedom, success, gratitude, and the ability to support others on their path. Allow these positive weeds to wholeheartedly cuddle your soul, mind, and body. These uplifting weeds will empower you to hug your uniqueness without feeling the need to emulate celebrities or others. Embrace your inner celebrity by rolling out your own red carpet, strutting with pride, and never seeing the end because it doesn't exist. You're one of a kind, so accept your uniqueness and avoid comparing yourself to others. The person you idolize may secretly desire to be in your shoes, so discover your true worth and let it sparkle.

During my childhood, I had a strong dislike for myself and longed to be like others. My skin color and facial features were unappealing to me. If children were offered plastic surgery, I'd have been the first to volunteer, even if it meant resembling a stranger. Just imagine if I had the surgery and now, as an adult, I've discovered my identity and nurtured a deep self-love within me. What do you think would occur?

In my opinion, self-love would not be sustained if I'd underwent surgery to change my appearance. Children are gullible and often try to conform to others, going to great lengths to fit in with the crowd.

The breathtaking natural beauty she witnessed astounded the woman on the train, but I failed to see what she saw. Witnessing a flower, she patiently anticipated hummingbirds to come by and engage in conversation with it. Unlike those who mocked me, the woman on the train recognized qualities in people that they didn't see in themselves. In order to comprehend what the woman on the train told me, my mindset had to change. Putting me down and shaming me was how the bullies coped with their own personal trauma.

The script given to me by the woman, stating, "you are beautiful and gorgeous," ignited a transformative shift in my mindset about myself, life, and my environment. Life doesn't always turn out how you expect. Moving to Canada helped me change my thinking and mindset, allowing me to grow into my true self. The affirmation I've been saying has transformed my life for the better. We're all distinct and extraordinary in our own ways. If you are reading this book, tell yourself you are beautiful and gorgeous.

10

"No one can make you feel inferior without your consent."
Eleanor Roosevelt

Seeking validation from others often leads us to feel inferior when they cannot bring us happiness. Take charge of your own life and make it better; don't give that power to others. Allowing others to control your mindset will keep you in a position of inferiority. I experienced feelings of inferiority as a child because of societal influence, and those feelings have persisted into my adult life. Shyness and low self-esteem devoured me. I had a desire to reveal myself to the world, but the negativity from my childhood held me back. The woman on the train helped in shattering my feelings of inferiority. Confidence was completely absent from my life. Occasionally, I would gaze into the mirror and notice all the things I disliked about my physical appearance, wondering why my nose wasn't straighter, my hair longer, my forehead smaller, or why I wasn't taller. My winning story was all about my constant complaints to God, my self-hate was deep, and I kept it to myself.

Instead of dwelling on negative self-image in the mirror, I started affirming my beauty after the train incident. Even on days when I doubted it, I kept repeating it and avoiding thoughts of wanting a straighter nose, longer hair, to be taller, and a smaller forehead. I kept building appreciation for my physical appearance as I repeated affirmations. If I could alter my belief, my inner appearance could also be transformed. I began affirming my strength by saying these affirmations and more: I am strong; I am beautiful; I am blessed.

Slowly, I saw a change in myself. People were giving me more compliments about my appearance, and I developed self-love. The affirmation had a positive impact, but it wasn't an overnight success. I spent years trying to believe the story I had constructed in my mind. These affirmations empowered me and boosted my self-esteem immensely. There were things I wished to pursue as a young girl, but I remained silent, fearing judgement and hurtful comments about my looks. The act of telling my story brought back my humanity. I fearlessly stepped into the world, reclaiming what was taken. Restoring my mindset and changing my belief system was something only I could accomplish. It was challenging, but I was determined to claim what was rightfully mine and fully embrace it. I realized I was giving too much power to others' words, so I made the choice to accept myself and embrace my goodness. The most challenging thing I ever had to do was learn to love myself, but it was also the most rewarding. I'm not concerned about what others say about me; I'm just being true to myself.

I have learned as an artist you just have to paint the image in your mind one brush stroke at a time, not changing it because someone doesn't like it. Don't wait for others to like it; it's your idea brought to life. When you have self-acceptance, it becomes simple to appreciate others and desire happiness. It took years for me to accept the degree of self-love that I had to work so hard for, solely for my validation, and not for others. Graduating and earning my love degree was crucial for moving forward and achieving success in life.

When someone says something negative, counter it with positive self-talk and reject the negativity. None of us should be made to feel inferior, as we are all children of the most high God. Our bodily processes are identical. Individuals without self-love view others as more important than themselves. True equality can only be achieved through self-love.

Society has shaped the belief that certain people's lives hold greater value, but inwardly they lack self-love. Being a millionaire or billionaire doesn't make you superior to anyone else. Your status may make it easy for you to navigate the world, but remember, you are still one out of billions of people. Lack of education, low self-esteem, and insecurity can contribute to feelings of inferiority. The story you tell yourself is where the significant changes can occur. The power to make decisions lies with you, not others.

It wasn't until later in life that I realized I had control over my existence, and it took me years to fully accept and sign my personal consent form. This consent began with the woman on the train, and it has required effort and belief in my story to cultivate genuine self-love. She helped ignite my belief system. I didn't know her personally. She was a stranger, who changed someone's life. Maybe she was sent for this one task to tell me that I was beautiful and gorgeous. Can you believe how amazing that is? To reassure me of my beauty, God had to send someone who didn't resemble me, for he made nothing that is unworthy. If someone who resembled me told me that I was beautiful and gorgeous, I might have doubted their sincerity because of my past experiences of bullying.

Refuse any invitation that aims to make you inferior. You are one of a kind, completely unique and irreplaceable in this world. Grant yourself permission to love and value yourself, and embrace your life journey, as you are the only one who can shape your narrative. Tell it from your perspective, not as a stranger would. Affirmation is a powerful tool to overcome barriers and I believe it can help you too, especially during challenges you may face. Remember, the stories we tell ourselves can impact our lives. We should tell ourselves positive stories and motivate others to do so, too.

If you can't offer words of encouragement to uplift and improve your life, please refrain from negativity, as words hold power when they enter our subconscious. If you come across a stranger, inform them of their beauty and offer a compliment—it could have a lasting impact on someone's life. Start your day by considering how you can improve someone's life with your positive attitude. Infect the world with your positivity and it will infect you in return.

As a child, I unintentionally granted bullies the power to make me feel inferior because of my ignorance. The tradition of valuing light skin over dark skin, a product of the subconscious mind rooted in the legacy of slavery, can only be challenged through the practice of self-love. It's challenging to uncover the truth when the lie has been camouflaged as the truth for so long. It took me years to escape the cycle of self-hate. It felt as if I was learning a new language in an unfamiliar location. When you have confidence in yourself, others can perceive your uniqueness and know that your self-value doesn't rely on external validation. Your importance is determined by factual proof, not by validation from others. Gain mastery over your own life. Take charge of your own mind and don't let others influence it.

QUESTION

1. Tell a stranger one positive compliment each day.

11

"You are enough. You have nothing to prove to anybody."
Maya Angelou

It would have been nice to realize in my youth that I was sufficient, but I'm content my journey has unfolded in this way. I had to experience different phases in my life to understand that I am complete and do not need to demonstrate anything to anyone. When I was a child, I wanted to alter my physical appearance because of my lack of knowledge. I'm grateful for the inner peace and self-love I've discovered within myself. The affirmations in my subconscious mind remain firmly stapled. Life is not a stroll through Central Park, devoid of horse manure, people, and dramatic moments. Life wouldn't be complete without the struggles and additional elements it brings. It will require effort to make it work exactly as we desire. We are our toughest critic, just like when the lady on the train told me, I was beautiful and gorgeous—I didn't understand what she saw in me. These words were spoken to me, intending to alter my perception of my authentic identity. It took me a long time to accept I was sufficient. When the belief finally solidified, I reflected on my childhood, questioning why I couldn't see the inner beauty. I allowed negativity to consume me, and it manifested in my life, making it difficult to break free. I had to reintroduce myself to myself, formulate a new character, but with massive loving, self-acceptance, positive language, and releasing toxic influences.

A stranger on the train assured me I was capable, but I had to convince myself of it. It may be told to you, but without action, it won't flourish.

I had to nurture the seed she'd planted in me, ensuring it grew with self-love and proper care so it could blossom into beautiful flowers. The seed that was planted in me as a child had to die slowly for the new seed to grow, without throne and thistle choking it. To thrive and fulfill its purpose, the seed must sometimes be moved from its current surroundings. The multitude of beauty standards I encountered in the media during my childhood made me doubt my worth. We often think that we must demonstrate our value to others in order to validate ourselves.

Having lived in Canada for a long time, I had friends from a wide range of cultures and ethnicities. I have this friend who is European American, and she doesn't have a positive view of herself. She would always complain that she was too pale, and the winters made it worse. She longed for some sunlight. Every week, she would go tanning. She was dissatisfied with her pale skin. This realization showed it's not just me who dislikes my dark skin; people from other ethnicities also struggle with their skin tone.

European American actors mostly dominated the movies I watched as a child on the island. I dreamt of pursuing a career in acting and singing, but my fear of being laughed at due to not having the skin of European Americans held me back. I kept my dreams to myself, fearing they would attract negativity. Being a person with dark skin, I believed TV wasn't for me. However, I found joy in performing for my family, singing, acting, and storytelling. These were the most memorable moments of my summer vacations.

Upon arriving in Canada, I had to set these dreams aside. I dedicated myself to self-reflection and self-exploration. Although struggles came with life in a new land, I didn't give up.

I was persistent in chasing my goals, even when the path seemed unclear. The journey of life is a constant source of valuable lessons. These are the lessons that shape us and help us develop resilience to keep moving forward. Reflecting on my childhood on the island, I realized the challenges of bullying and self-hate shaped my life. All things happen when they should.

On the train, a woman told me a story I should have been telling myself—falling in love with who I am and not letting others define me. I find joy in both living life to the fullest and supporting others on their path to make a difference in the world. We fail to examine our position on this earth due to our intricately woven uniqueness. Each of us is a masterpiece, made in God's image, unlike anyone else. Should I manage to find the lady who disappeared from the train at the next station, I would disclose the true story of my life and the transformative effect she unknowingly had on it. Remember, change doesn't happen overnight, so stay persistent. The reward will become evident if you start with tiny habits. Your transformative event may not mirror mine but remember other narratives share more similarities than differences. Create beautiful narratives about yourself, because storytelling is ingrained in our culture. Hearing stories from others is something we love, especially when they have a happy ending. Tell yourself stories with happy endings that have the power to change your life.

Have the courage to put yourself first, take risks, believe in your abilities, and take control of your own life.

Start your life journey with daily affirmations:

- I am strong.

- I am a child of God.

- I am healthy.

- I am confident.

- I am courageous.

- I am successful.

- Today is going to be a great day.

- I am grateful and thankful for life.

- I love myself.

- I am enough.

- I am bold and brave.

Thank you for reading this book. I hope it moves you to make changes and to love yourself.

https://open.spotify.com/track/1MBkQXMTSc2H RSwygMpBbe

https://music.apple.com/us/album/beautiful-and-gorgeous-everyday-single/1702483698

www.cleannejohnson.com

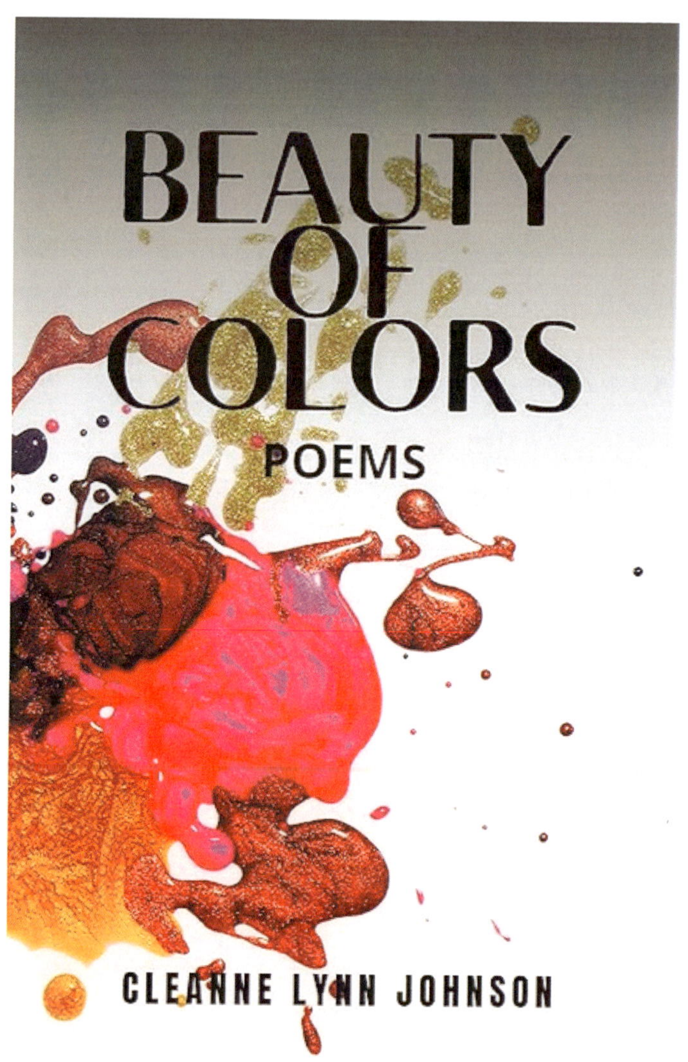
BEAUTY
OF
COLORS
POEMS
CLEANNE LYNN JOHNSON

Beauty
of Life
1 0 1
Inspirational Quotes
Cleanne Lynn Johnson

LOVE MY COLORS

Why
THIS TRIP
CLEANNE LYNN JOHNSON